2019 Guide for Points-Based Skilled Independent Migrants to Australia

Ng Chee Min

Published in Australia in 2019
by CMN & Associates

Copyright © Chee Min Ng 2019

The right of Chee Min Ng to be identified as the author of this work has been asserted by him in accordance with the Copyright Amendment (Moral Rights) Act 2000.

This book is copyright. Except as permitted under the Copyright Act 1968, no part my be reproduced, copies, scanned, stored in a retrieval system, recorded or transmitted in any form or by any means without prior written permission.

The contents are for information only and not to be treated as professional advice. Although the author and publisher have made every effort to ensure that the information in this book was correct at press time, the author and publisher make no representation or warranties with respect to the accuracy, applicability or completeness of the contents of this book.

2019 Guide for Points-Based Skilled Independent Migrants to Australia
ISBN: 978-0-9923035-6-3

Other books by the author
Emigrating: Going to Australia
Australia Skilled Migration In A Nutshell
Australia - Migrant Success Stories
Forthcoming
So You Want to Emigrate? LET'S LOOK AT AUSTRALIA
Living in Australia - Guide for Would-Be Migrants

From The Author

"What is life like in Australia?"
"How can I migrate to Australia?"

I am often asked these questions by visitors to Australia and by others during my trips overseas. This motivated me to write my first book *Emigrating: Going to Australia*. Since then, I have written many books on the subject.

This book covers the Skilled Independent (subclass 189) visa – Points-tested stream, a major category of the Australian Points-based skilled migration program.

The book addresses the following key questions for aspiring skilled independent migrants:

What are the eligibility requirements and the visa-holder's entitlements under subclass 189 visa?
What are the hurdles/steps to reach the final outcome?

The information on visa requirements, visa-holders' entitlements for the various migration subclasses is based on the current 2018-19 requirements.

Chee Min
Australia
21 February 2019

Contents

1. Overview — 7
About Skilled Independent Visa — 7
Eligibility Criteria — 7
Visa-holder's Entitlements — 7
Visa Application — 8

2. Eligibility Criteria — 9
Age < 45 years — 9
Nominated occupation — 9
Skilled occupation lists (SOL) — 9
Positive skills assessment — 10
Points Test — 10
English language proficiency — 10
Health requirements — 11
Character requirement — 11
Outstanding debts to Australian government — 11
Australian values statement — 12
No cancellation of visa previously or refusal of visa application — 12

3. Skills Assessment — 13
Nominated occupation — 13
Positive skills assessment — 13
Skills assessing authorities — 13
The assessment process — 13
Arranging for skills assessment — 14
Appeal against the assessment outcome — 14
Information and supporting documents required by assessment authorities — 14

4. Expression of Interest (EOI) — 15
How is invitation to apply issued? — 15
Why is information provided in EOI is important? — 15
EOI in three simple steps — 15
Some FAQs — 16

5. Visa Application — 18
Important to provide true information — 18
Consequences of providing bogus document or false and misleading information — 18
Supporting information and documentary proof — 18

Visa application in 5 steps	19
Check the ImmiAccount regularly	19
Visa application fees	19
Other costs visa applicants should budget for	19
Visa processing time	20
Some FAQs	20

Factsheets

Factsheet 2.1 2018-19 Combined Current Skills Occupation Lists	22
Factsheet 2.2 Points Test Table	35
Factsheet 2.3 Australian Values Statement	36
Factsheet 3.1 Skills Assessing Authorities	37
Factsheet 4.1 Occupation Ceilings 2018-19	38
Factsheet 5.1 Personal, Relationship Information & Documents	41
Factsheet 5.2 Skills, Qualification, Experience, English Proficiency & Skills Assessments	42
Factsheet 5.3 Health & Character Requirements	43
Factsheet 5.4 Partner's Documents	44
Factsheet 5.5 Dependents Under 18 - Documentary Proof	45
Factsheet 5.6 Dependents Over 18 – Documentary Proof	46
Factsheet 5.7 Skills Assessment Documentary Proof	47
Factsheet 5.8 Expression of Interest Documentary Proof	48
Factsheet 5.9 Non-English Documents & Document Scanning	49
Factsheet 5.10 If Applicant is getting Help	50
About the Author	**51**

1. Overview

About Skilled Independent Visa

Skilled Independent (subclass 189) visa

This is a permanent residence visa for skilled workers who are not sponsored by employer, relative, or nominated by state or territory government.

2018-19 available places

The 2018-19 planned skilled intakes for skilled independent visas are 43,990 places.

Eligibility Criteria

What are the eligibility criteria?

Applicants need to have a minimum point-score (currently 65) in addition to meeting the other requirements.

Points are assigned for age, qualification, experience, English proficiency level, nomination, study in Australia, partner's qualifications and experience and other requirements.

The eligibility criteria are covered in greater details in Chapter 2.

Visa-holder's Entitlements

Permanent residence

Sub-class 189 is a permanent residence visas allowing the visa-holder indefinite stay in Australia.

Medicare benefits

Visa-holders are eligible to Medicare (the national health scheme) benefits.

Social security benefits

Visa-holders are eligible to most social security benefits though some benefits, e.g. unemployment benefits are available after a qualifying period and subjected to means test.

Sponsor eligible family members

Permanent residents after two years in Australia are eligible to sponsor eligible relatives for permanent resident application.

Australian citizenship

Permanent residents can apply for citizenship after having lived in Australia for five years and meeting the citizenship requirements.

Visa Application

Expression of interest (EOI)

Interested candidates first lodge an expression of interest (EOI) with SkillSelect – an online portal of the Department of Home Affairs (DHA).

SkillSelect generates invitations to apply to eligible candidates based on the information furnished.

Expression of interest is covered in Chapter 4.

Apply for visa

Candidates apply for the visa only when invited by SkillSelect.

Candidates have 60 days to submit their visa applications via SkillSelect.

Visa-outcome

SkillSelect informs applicants of their application outcome.

Visa application is covered in Chapter 5.

2. Eligibility Criteria

Age < 45 years

Applicant has to be aged less than 45 to be invited to apply for the visa.

Applicant can still apply for the visa if applicant turns 45 after receiving invitation to apply.

Applicant turns 45 after submitting the EOI but before DHA's invitation to apply will not receive an invite.

Nominated occupation

All intending skilled migrants will need to nominate an occupation that best matches his or her qualifications and skills on the relevant skilled occupation list applicable to the visa subclass.

Skilled occupation lists (SOL)

These are skills lists detailing the skilled occupations eligible for intending migrants to Australia to nominate an occupation for skilled migration purpose.

The occupation lists, with nominated occupations and appropriate ANZSCO code, are updated regularly to reflect the skills that Australia needs.

> **ANZSCO code**
>
> The Australian and New Zealand Standard Classification of Occupations (ANZSCO) started as a joint development project of the Australian Bureau of Statistics (ABS), Statistics New Zealand (Statistics NZ) and the Australian Government Department of Education, Employment and Workplace Relations for use in the collection, publication and analysis of occupation statistics.

The skilled occupation lists applicable for 2018-19 Skilled Independent (subclass 189) is DHA's Medium and Long-term Strategic Skills List (MLTSS).

The occupations available for nomination for skilled migration for 2018-19 are in Factsheet 2.1 Combined Current List of Eligible Skilled Occupations at the end of this chapter.

Positive skills assessment

Applicants need to obtain a positive skills assessment of their qualification, skills and experience in relation to the nominated occupation.

Skills assessment is covered in Chapter 3.

Points Test

Points test score of at least 65 points is a requirement for all applicants.

Points are assigned for:

- Age
- Qualification
- Experience
- English proficiency level
- Study in Australia
- Partner's qualifications and experience
- Other requirements

Factsheet 2.2 Points Test lists the points score assigned to the various categories.

English language proficiency

Applicants need to have a COMPETENT English proficiency level.

The following English language tests are accepted for the purpose of determining the proficiency levels:

- International English Language Testing System (IELTS)
- Test of English as a Foreign Language internet-Based Test (TOFEL iBT)
- Pearson Test of English (PTE)
- Academic Cambridge English: Advanced (CAE) test
- Occupational English Test (OET)

Competent level of English for the various English language tests are as listed below:

- IELTS 6 in each component
- TOEFL iBT 12 for listening, 13 for reading, 21 for writing and 18 for speaking
- PTE Academic 50+ in each component

❖ Cambridge (CAE) 169+ in each component test taken after 1/1/2015

Passport holders of UK, USA, Ireland, Canada or NZ are considered to have met the required English proficiency level.

Candidate with a higher proficiency level, e.g. proficiency and superior levels, will receive a higher points score in the Points Test.

Factsheet 2.3 English Proficiency Levels lists the details of the various levels of English proficiency.

Health requirements

All visa applicants, i.e. the main applicant, secondary applicants and any dependents have to satisfy the health requirements.

The DHA will inform the applicant when to arrange the health examinations for the applicant and the accompanying family members.

The health requirements vary according to applicant's age as shown in Factsheet 2.4 Health Requirements.

Character requirement

All visa applicants, i.e. the main applicant, secondary applicants and any dependents have to satisfy the character requirements.

Police certificates are required as part of the character requirement.

The DHA will inform offshore applicant to obtain police certificates for the applicant and each of the dependents (whether migrating or not) aged 16 years or older from each country the applicant and the family members have lived in for 12 months or more over the last 10 years or for those below 26 years old, since they turned 16.

Onshore applicant who has been in Australia for 12 months or longer is required to provide an Australian National Police Check when submitting the visa application.

All visa applicants must advise DHA if they have any criminal convictions inside or outside of Australia.

Visa application may be refused or visa cancelled for non-disclosure.

The character requirements are listed in Factsheet 2.5 Character Requirements.

Outstanding debts to Australian government

Applicants must have repaid or have made arrangement to repay outstanding debts to Australian government.

Australian values statement

Applicants have to sign the Australian Value Statement as detailed in Factsheet 3.6 Australian Value Statement.

No cancellation of visa previously or refusal of visa application

Applicant must not have visa previously cancelled or application refused.

3. Skills Assessment

Nominated occupation

All intending skilled migrants will need to nominate an occupation that **best matches** his or her qualifications and skills on the relevant skilled occupation list applicable to the visa subclass.

Positive skills assessment

All interested candidates for subclass 189 visa need to have their qualifications and experience assessed.

They have to obtain a positive assessment from the relevant assessing authority.

> **Importance of positive skills assessment**
>
> Intending skilled migrants should remember that positive skills assessment is **Hurdle #1** in their skilled visa application journey.
>
> Applicant should spend sufficient time on gathering the documents and information.
>
> Good amount of effort should also be devoted to have a clear and convincing presentation.

Skills assessing authorities

The relevant assessing authority for nominated occupation will usually be able to determine the individual's qualifications are of a standard that is comparable to a relevant Australian qualification in the case of applicants with qualifications from overseas.

A listing of skills assessing authorities is in Factsheet 3.1 Skills Assessing Authorities.

The assessment process

Skills assessing authorities determine whether the applicant's qualifications and work experience are at the required level and closely related to the nominated occupation (ANZSCO).

While individual assessing authority has its assessing procedures, the following steps are indicative of the assessment process.

AQF comparability

Candidate's qualifications are assessed to establish the AQF comparability basing on Australian national education standards.

Course units assessment

The course units are assessed to determine whether the content is adequate.

Assessment in relation to nominated occupation

This involves assessing the course units in relation to the nominated occupation as per the ANZSCO Code Information document

Determine relevant experience required

This involves establish the relevant work experience required.

Arranging for skills assessment

Individuals will need to contact the relevant assessing authorities to have their skills assessed as suitable for the nominated occupations.

To assist applicants in nominating an occupation, the assessing authorities in most instances will provide information and example of course units and employment duties for each occupation.

Skills assessing authority charge fees for assessment and also for review and appeal.

Appeal against the assessment outcome

There are processes in place for candidates to request a review and appeal for any negative skills assessment outcome.

A review application is normally has to be made within a timeframe on receipt of the assessment outcome.

Candidates may also wish to change the nominated occupation (ANZSCO) or include additional work experience or qualifications.

Information and supporting documents required by assessment authorities

Factsheet 3.2 gives an indication of the type of information and supporting documents required by an assessing authority.

4. Expression of Interest (EOI)

How is invitation to apply issued?

SkillSelect issues invitations to apply to eligible candidates based on the information furnished in their expression of interest.

EOI – An important Hurdle
SkillSelect issues invitations to apply to eligible candidates based on the information furnished in their expression of interest.

Why is information provided in EOI is important?

It is important as candidate, when invited to apply for the visa subclass, has to provide **Documentary Proof** for all that is provided in the EOI.

The proof includes the following if applicable:

- Skills assessment
- English language skills
- Skilled employment
- Qualifications
- Australian study requirement
- State or territory government agency nomination
- Specialist education requirement
- Accredited community language
- Study in regional Australia
- Partner skills
- Professional year in Australia

EOI in three simple steps

Create an account

Candidate creates an EOI online via SkillSelect by:

- Enter personal information
- Confirm information provided
- Create an account by providing email address and password
- SkillSelect will email an EOI Identification Number

Sign-in with EOI Identification Number and password

- Select visa type
- Provide English language test details
- Provide education and qualifications details
- Provide skills assessment details
- Provide employment history

❖ Declare and submit

Download EOI
❖ View EOI
❖ View Points breakdown

Some FAQs

What should the candidate be aware of?

Candidates for all points-based skilled visas have to complete the skills assessment points test section.

Candidate should ensure that the information provided is correct and there are supporting documents to substantiate the information.

Will an individual able to complete the EOI if the points-score is less than the minimum score of 65?

Candidates will be able to complete the EOI even if they have less than the 65 minimum points.

However, they will not be invited to apply for a visa.

Is there any fee payable?

There is no fee payable when submitting an EOI.

How long is candidate's Expression of interest (EOI) valid?

The completed EOI is stored via SkillSelect and is valid for two years.

What happen if an EOI is incomplete?

Incomplete EOIs will be stored for two years but will not receive an invitation to apply.

Can the candidate update the EOI?

Individuals can update, on SkillSelect website, their information in the EOI anytime during the period provided they haven't received an invitation to apply.

Candidates may want to reflect changes in work experience, higher qualification acquired, improvement in English language ability and change in family composition.

Is there a response that the EOI has been received?

Once the EOI has been lodged, an EOI record of response is issued to candidate.

The record of response details the personal, education, English and employment details as submitted by the candidate.

Does SkillSelect update candidates of the progress of their EOI?

SkillSelect does not notify candidates of the progress of their EOI or their chances of receiving an invitation.

How do candidates know their chances of receiving an EOI?

The Department publishes the lowest points scoring points test mark that an invitation to apply was based after each invitation round.

This provides candidates an indication of the chances for receiving an invitation in future rounds.

What are the possible outcomes on EOI application?

Candidates might receive invitation, in the case of subclass 189 candidates, from SkillSelect, to lodge the visa application. EOI are issued automatically subject to occupation ceilings.

What are annual occupation ceilings?

Annual occupation ceilings on the number of invitation issued for an occupation group apply to Skilled Independent visa (subclass 189) and Skilled Regional (Provisional) visa (subclass 489).

Factsheet 4.1 Occupation Ceilings 2018-2019 lists the occupation ceilings for the affected occupations.

When will a candidate's EOI be removed?

A candidate's EOI will be removed from the database if the candidate fails to lodge a visa application after two invitations to apply have been issued or candidate has since been granted a visa.

5. Visa Application

Important to provide true information

DHA may refuse applicant's visa application if applicant provides a bogus document or information that is false or misleading or if applicant cannot prove his/her identity.

DHA can refuse applicant's visa application if the applicant or a member of applicant's family provide:

- ❖ A bogus document or information that is false or misleading relating to a visa application
- ❖ Has given DHA a bogus document or information that is false or misleading relating to any visa you held in the 12 months before applicant applied for this visa

Consequences of providing bogus document or false and misleading information

If DHA refuses the application because applicant provided a bogus document or information that is false or misleading, DHA:

- ❖ Will not grant applicant any other visa for 3 years
- ❖ Might refuse any current visa applications by members of applicant's family
- ❖ Might not grant applicant's family members a visa for 3 years

Supporting information and documentary proof

Please refer to the following factsheets on the requirements:

- ❖ Factsheet 5.1 Personal, Relationship Information & Documents
- ❖ Factsheet 5.2 Skills, Qualification, Experience, English Proficiency & Skills Assessments
- ❖ Factsheet 5.3 Health & Character Requirements
- ❖ Factsheet 5.4 Partner's Documents
- ❖ Factsheet 5.5 Dependents Under 18 - Documentary Proof
- ❖ Factsheet 5.6 Dependents Over 18 – Documentary Proof
- ❖ Factsheet 5.7 Skills Assessment Documentary Proof
- ❖ Factsheet 5.8 Expression of Interest Documentary Proof
- ❖ Factsheet 5.9 Non-English Documents & Document Scanning
- ❖ Factsheet 5.10 If Applicant is getting Help

Visa application in 5 steps

- Log into SkillSelect account, select/click Apply for visa to get onto ImmiAccount.
- Log in or create an ImmiAccount.
- Attach the required documents.
- Pay the application fee.
- Record the transaction reference number (TRN).

DHA will confirm on receipt of the application.

Check the ImmiAccount regularly

Applicant has to regularly check applicant's ImmiAccount.

It's in the applicant's interest to regularly check ImmiAccount of any request for information from DHA.

Visa application fees

The initial non-refundable fees for subclass 189 payable on lodging the visa application are:

- Main applicant - $3,755
- Additional applicant age ≥ 18 - $1,875 per person
- Accompanying child age <18 - $945 per person

For successful applicant, a second visa application payment of $4,885 is payable after the visa applicant's accompanying family member ages 18 and over has been assessed as not having functional English.

This fee entitles them to English class under the Adult Migrant English Program (AMEP) in Australia.

Other costs visa applicants should budget for

Applicant should also factor in the following costs:

- Medical examination cost - payable directly to the doctor conducting the examination
- Character clearance (police check) - payable directly to the police of those countries
- Certification/translation of documents - payable to translator
- Migration agent (if one is used) - Fee ranges from $4,000 - $6,000 or more depending on case and migration agent*
- Other costs

If applicable. Many applicants do not engage the service of a migration agent.

Visa processing time

The processing time is dependent on application volumes, case complexity and completeness of the applications.

DHA updates and displays the visa processing time online monthly. It display two processing times in calendar days – one for 75% of applications and the other for 90% of the applications.

The latest processing time for Skilled Independent subclass 189 skilled visas is as follow:

- 75% - 5 months
- 90% - 7 months

Some FAQs

Does DHA provide regular updates?

DHA does not provide updates on application within the standard processing time.

Is DHA obliged to request for further information?

However, DHA is not obliged to request for further information or documents and may make a decision on application without requesting more documents.

What about health examinations?

DHA will let applicant know of health examinations if applicant didn't have them before the application.

DHA might ask for applicant's biometrics.

What about sending remaining documents?

Complete sending all documents by attaching any remaining documents in ImmiAccount.

How does the applicant notify DHA of mistakes on application?

Applicant must inform DHA as soon as possible of any mistake/s on the application by completing *Form 1023 Notification of incorrect answers* and attach it to the application in ImmiAccount.

How to notify DHA of changes?

Applicant will need to notify the department of the following:

- Changes to phone number, email, address or passport
- Changes to marital or de facto status

- ❖ Birth of a child
- ❖ Withdrawal of application

How to add new family members?

This can be done after the application but before DHA decide on the visa application by completing and attaching *Form 1436 Adding an additional applicant* after lodgement in ImmiAccount and pay the visa application fee for new members.

Health and character requirements apply to the family members added.

How will DHA inform visa applicants of outcome?

Applicant will be informed of visa outcome in writing.

The visa grant for successful applicant will contain the visa grant number, commencement date of visa and visa conditions, if applicable.

Will unsuccessful applicant get a refund of visa application fee?

Unsuccessful applicant will be provided with reason for refusal and whether the applicant has a right to a review of the decision.

There will be no refund of application fee.

Factsheet 2.1 2018-19 Combined Current Skills Occupation Lists

Example: Actuary/224111/MLTSSL/VETASSESS

Actuary – occupation
22411 – ANSCO Occupation Group Code
MLTSSL – Medium Long-Term Strategic Skill List
STSOL – Short-Term Skilled Occupation List
VETASSESS – Assessing authority

Accommodation and Hospitality Managers nec/141999/STSOL/VETASSESS
Accountant (General)/221111/MLTSSL/CAANZ/CPAA/IPA
Actuary/224111/MLTSSL/VETASSESS
Acupuncturist/252211/STSOL/Chinese Medicine Board of Australia
Advertising Manager/131113/STSOL/AIM
Advertising Specialist/225111/STSOL/VETASSESS
Aeronautical Engineer/233911/MLTSSL/Engineers Australia
Aeroplane Pilot/231111/Regional/CASA
Agricultural Consultant/234111/MLTSSL/VETASSESS
Agricultural Engineer/233912/MLTSSL/Engineers Australia
Agricultural Scientist/234112/MLTSSL/VETASSESS
Agricultural Technician/311111/Regional/VETASSESS
Airconditioning and Mechanical Services Plumber/334112/MLTSSL/TRA
Airconditioning and Refrigeration Mechanic/342111/MLTSSL/TRA
Aircraft Maintenance Engineer (Avionics)/323111/STSOL/TRA
Aircraft Maintenance Engineer (Mechanical)/323112/STSOL/TRA
Aircraft Maintenance Engineer (Structures)/323113/STSOL/TRA
Ambulance Officer/411111/STSOL/VETASSESS
Amusement Centre Manager/149111/Regional/VETASSESS
Anaesthetic Technician/311211/STSOL/VETASSESS
Anaesthetist/253211/STSOL/MedBA
Analyst Programmer/261311/MLTSSL/ACS
Animal Attendants and Trainers nec/361199/STSOL/VETASSESS
Apiarist/121311/STSOL/VETASSESS
Aquaculture Farmer/121111/STSOL/VETASSESS
Arborist/362212/STSOL/TRA
Architect/232111/MLTSSL/AACA
Architectural Draftsperson/312111/STSOL/VETASSESS
Architectural, Building and Surveying Technicians nec/312199/STSOL/VETASSESS
Art Teacher (Private Tuition)/249211/STSOL/VETASSESS

Artistic Director/212111/STSOL/VETASSESS
Arts Administrator or Manager/139911/STSOL/VETASSESS
Audiologist/252711/MLTSSL/VETASSESS
Automotive Electrician/321111/MLTSSL/TRA
Baker/351111/STSOL/TRA
Barrister/271111/MLTSSL/A legal admissions authority of a State or Territory
Beef Cattle Farmer/121312/STSOL/VETASSESS
Biochemist/234513/MLTSSL/VETASSESS
Biomedical Engineer/233913/MLTSSL/Engineers Australia
Biotechnologist/234514/MLTSSL/VETASSESS
Boat Builder and Repairer/399111/MLTSSL/TRA
Book or Script Editor/212212/STSOL/VETASSESS
Botanist/234515/MLTSSL/VETASSESS
Bricklayer/331111/MLTSSL/TRA
Building and Engineering Technicians nec/312999/Regional/VETASSESS/Engineers Australia
Building Inspector/312113/STSOL/VETASSESS
Business Machine Mechanic/342311/STSOL/TRA
Butcher or Smallgoods Maker/351211/STSOL/TRA
Cabinetmaker/394111/MLTSSL/TRA
Cabler (Data and Telecommunications)/342411/STSOL/TRA
Cafe or Restaurant Manager/141111/STSOL/VETASSESS
Camera Operator (Film, Television or Video)/399512/STSOL/TRA
Caravan Park and Camping Ground Manager/141211/Regional/VETASSESS
Cardiac Technician/311212/STSOL/VETASSESS
Cardiologist/253312/MLTSSL/MedBA
Cardiothoracic Surgeon/253512/MLTSSL/MedBA
Careers Counsellor/272111/STSOL/VETASSESS
Carpenter/331212/MLTSSL/TRA
Carpenter and Joiner/331211/MLTSSL/TRA
Cartographer/232213/MLTSSL/VETASSESS
Chef/351311/MLTSSL/TRA
Chemical Engineer/233111/MLTSSL/Engineers Australia
Chemical Plant Operator/399211/STSOL/TRA
Chemist/234211/MLTSSL/VETASSESS
Chemistry Technician/311411/STSOL/VETASSESS
Chief Executive or Managing Director/111111/MLTSSL/AIM
Chief Information Officer/135111/MLTSSL/ACS
Child Care Centre Manager/134111/MLTSSL/TRA
Chiropractor/252111/MLTSSL/CCEA
Cinema or Theatre Manager/149912/Regional/VETASSESS

Civil Engineer/233211/MLTSSL/Engineers Australia
Civil Engineering Draftsperson/312211/MLTSSL/Engineers Australia/ VETASSESS
Civil Engineering Technician/312212/MLTSSL/VETASSESS
Clinical Coder/599915/Regional/VETASSESS
Clinical Haematologist/253313/MLTSSL/MedBA
Clinical Psychologist/272311/MLTSSL/APS
Commodities Trader/222111/STSOL/VETASSESS
Community Arts Worker/272611/Regional/VETASSESS
Community Worker/411711/STSOL/ACWA
Company Secretary/221211/STSOL/VETASSESS
Complementary Health Therapists nec/252299/STSOL/VETASSESS
Computer Network and Systems Engineer/263111/MLTSSL/ACS
Conference and Event Organiser/149311/STSOL/VETASSESS
Conservation Officer/234311/Regional/VETASSESS
Conservator/234911/MLTSSL/VETASSESS
Construction Estimator/312114/Regional/VETASSESS
Construction Project Manager/133111/MLTSSL/VETASSESS
Contract Administrator/511111/STSOL/VETASSESS
Cook/351411/STSOL/TRA
Copywriter/212411/STSOL/VETASSESS
Corporate General Manager/111211/MLTSSL/AIM
Corporate Services Manager/132111/STSOL/VETASSESS
Cotton Grower/121211/STSOL/VETASSESS
Counsellors nec/272199/STSOL/VETASSESS
Crop Farmers nec/121299/STSOL/VETASSESS
Customer Service Manager/149212/STSOL/VETASSESS
Dairy Cattle Farmer/121313/STSOL/VETASSESS
Dance Teacher (Private Tuition)/249212/STSOL/VETASSESS
Dancer or Choreographer/211112/STSOL/VETASSESS
Database Administrator/262111/STSOL/ACS
Dental Hygienist/411211/Regional/VETASSESS
Dental Specialist/252311/STSOL/ADC
Dental Technician/411213/STSOL/TRA
Dental Therapist/411214/Regional/VETASSESS
Dentist/252312/STSOL/ADC
Dermatologist/253911/MLTSSL/MedBA
Developer Programmer/261312/MLTSSL/ACS
Diagnostic and Interventional Radiologist/253917/MLTSSL/MedBA
Diesel Motor Mechanic/321212/MLTSSL/TRA
Dietitian/251111/STSOL/DAA
Director (Film, Television, Radio or Stage)/212312/STSOL/VETASSESS

Disabilities Services Officer/411712/STSOL/VETASSESS
Diversional Therapist/411311/STSOL/VETASSESS
Diving Instructor (Open Water)/452311/STSOL/VETASSESS
Dog Handler or Trainer/361111/STSOL/VETASSESS
Drainer/334113/MLTSSL/TRA
Dressmaker or Tailor/393213/STSOL/TRA
Driving Instructor/451211/Regional/VETASSESS
Drug and Alcohol Counsellor/272112/STSOL/VETASSESS
Early Childhood (Pre-primary School) Teacher/241111/MLTSSL/AITSL
Earth Science Technician/311412/STSOL/VETASSESS
Economist/224311/MLTSSL/VETASSESS
Education Adviser/249111/STSOL/VETASSESS
Education Managers nec/134499/STSOL/VETASSESS
Educational Psychologist/272312/MLTSSL/APS
Electrical Engineer/233311/MLTSSL/Engineers Australia
Electrical Engineering Draftsperson/312311/MLTSSL/Engineers Australia
Electrical Engineering Technician/312312/MLTSSL/TRA
Electrical Linesworker/342211/Regional/TRA
Electrician (General)/341111/MLTSSL/TRA
Electrician (Special Class)/341112/MLTSSL/TRA
Electronic Equipment Trades Worker/342313/MLTSSL/TRA
Electronic Instrument Trades Worker (General)/342314/MLTSSL/TRA
Electronic Instrument Trades Worker (Special Class)/342315/MLTSSL/TRA
Electronics Engineer/233411/MLTSSL/Engineers Australia
Emergency Medicine Specialist/253912/MLTSSL/MedBA
Emergency Service Worker/441211/Regional/VETASSESS
Endocrinologist/253315/MLTSSL/MedBA
Engineering Manager/133211/MLTSSL/Engineers Australia/AIM
Engineering Professionals nec/233999/MLTSSL/Engineers Australia
Engineering Technologist/233914/MLTSSL/Engineers Australia
Enrolled Nurse/411411/STSOL/ANMAC
Environmental Consultant/234312/MLTSSL/VETASSESS
Environmental Engineer/233915/MLTSSL/Engineers Australia
Environmental Health Officer/251311/Regional/VETASSESS
Environmental Manager/139912/MLTSSL/VETASSESS
Environmental Research Scientist/234313/MLTSSL/VETASSESS
Environmental Scientists nec/234399/MLTSSL/VETASSESS
Exercise Physiologist/234915/Regional/VETASSESS
External Auditor/221213/MLTSSL/CAANZ/CPAA/IPA
Facilities Manager/149913/STSOL/VETASSESS

Faculty Head/134411/MLTSSL/VETASSESS
Family and Marriage Counsellor/272113/STSOL/VETASSESS
Family Support Worker/411713/STSOL/VETASSESS
Farrier/322113/STSOL/TRA
Fashion Designer/232311/STSOL/VETASSESS
Fibrous Plasterer/333211/MLTSSL/TRA
Film and Video Editor/212314/STSOL/VETASSESS
Finance Broker/222112/STSOL/VETASSESS
Finance Manager/132211/STSOL/CAANZ/CPAA/IPA
Financial Brokers nec/222199/STSOL/VETASSESS
Financial Dealers nec/222299/STSOL/VETASSESS
Financial Institution Branch Manager/149914/Regional/VETASSESS
Financial Investment Adviser/222311/STSOL/VETASSESS
Financial Investment Manager/222312/STSOL/VETASSESS
Financial Market Dealer/222211/STSOL/VETASSESS
First Aid Trainer/451815/Regional/VETASSESS
Fitness Centre Manager/149112/Regional/VETASSESS
Fitter (General)/323211/MLTSSL/TRA
Fitter and Turner/323212/MLTSSL/TRA
Fitter-Welder/323213/MLTSSL/TRA
Flight Attendant/451711/Regional/VETASSESS
Floor Finisher/332111/Regional/TRA
Florist/362111/STSOL/TRA
Flower Grower/121212/STSOL/VETASSESS
Flying Instructor/231113/Regional/VETASSESS
Food Technologist/234212/MLTSSL/VETASSESS
Footballer/452411/STSOL/VETASSESS
Forester/234113/MLTSSL/VETASSESS
Fruit or Nut Grower/121213/STSOL/VETASSESS
Funeral Workers nec/451399/Regional/VETASSESS
Furniture Finisher/394211/STSOL/TRA
Gallery or Museum Curator/224212/STSOL/VETASSESS
Gardener (General)/362211/STSOL/TRA
Gas or Petroleum Operator/399212/Regional/TRA
Gasfitter/334114/MLTSSL/TRA
Gastroenterologist/253316/MLTSSL/MedBA
General Practitioner/253111/MLTSSL/MedBA
Geologist/234411/STSOL/VETASSESS
Geophysicist/234412/MLTSSL/VETASSESS
Geotechnical Engineer/233212/MLTSSL/Engineers Australia
Glazier/333111/MLTSSL/TRA
Grain, Oilseed or Pasture Grower/121214/STSOL/VETASSESS
Grape Grower/121215/STSOL/VETASSESS

Graphic Designer/232411/STSOL/VETASSESS
Greenkeeper/362311/STSOL/TRA
Gymnastics Coach or Instructor/452312/STSOL/VETASSESS
Hairdresser/391111/STSOL/TRA
Hardware Technician/313111/STSOL/TRA
Health and Welfare Services Managers nec/134299/STSOL/VETASSESS
Health Diagnostic and Promotion Professionals nec/251999/STSOL/VETASSESS
Health Information Manager/224213/STSOL/VETASSESS
Health Promotion Officer/251911/STSOL/VETASSESS
Helicopter Pilot/231114/Regional/CASA
Horse Breeder/121316/Regional/VETASSESS
Horse Riding Coach or Instructor/452313/STSOL/VETASSESS
Horse Trainer/361112/MLTSSL/TRA
Hospital Pharmacist/251511/STSOL/APharmC
Hotel or Motel Manager/141311/STSOL/VETASSESS
Human Resource Adviser/223111/Regional/VETASSESS
Human Resource Manager/132311/STSOL/AIM
Hydrogeologist/234413/MLTSSL/VETASSESS
ICT Account Manager/225211/STSOL/VETASSESS
ICT Business Analyst/261111/MLTSSL/ACS
ICT Business Development Manager/225212/STSOL/VETASSESS
ICT Customer Support Officer/313112/STSOL/TRA
ICT Managers nec/135199/STSOL/ACS
ICT Project Manager/135112/STSOL/ACS
ICT Quality Assurance Engineer/263211/STSOL/ACS
ICT Sales Representative/225213/STSOL/VETASSESS
ICT Security Specialist/262112/MLTSSL/ACS
ICT Support and Test Engineers nec/263299/STSOL/ACS
ICT Support Engineer/263212/STSOL/ACS
ICT Support Technicians nec/313199/STSOL/TRA
ICT Systems Test Engineer/263213/STSOL/ACS
ICT Trainer/223211/STSOL/ACS
Illustrator/232412/STSOL/VETASSESS
Industrial Designer/232312/STSOL/VETASSESS
Industrial Engineer/233511/MLTSSL/Engineers Australia
Industrial Pharmacist/251512/STSOL/VETASSESS
Information and Organisation Professionals nec/224999/STSOL/VETASSESS
Insurance Agent/611211/STSOL/VETASSESS
Insurance Broker/222113/STSOL/VETASSESS
Insurance Loss Adjuster/599612/STSOL/VETASSESS

Intellectual Property Lawyer/271214/Regional/VETASSESS
Intensive Care Ambulance Paramedic/411112/STSOL/VETASSESS
Intensive Care Specialist/253317/MLTSSL/MedBA
Interior Designer/232511/STSOL/VETASSESS
Internal Auditor/221214/MLTSSL/VETASSESS
Interpreter/272412/STSOL/NAATI
Jeweller/399411/STSOL/TRA
Jewellery Designer/232313/STSOL/VETASSESS
Jockey/452413/Regional/TRA
Joiner/331213/MLTSSL/TRA
Journalists and Other Writers nec/212499/STSOL/VETASSESS
Judicial and Other Legal Professionals nec/271299/STSOL/VETASSESS
Laboratory Manager/139913/STSOL/VETASSESS
Land Economist/224511/MLTSSL/VETASSESS
Landscape Architect/232112/MLTSSL/VETASSESS
Landscape Gardener/362213/STSOL/TRA
Liaison Officer/224912/Regional/VETASSESS
Librarian/224611/STSOL/VETASSESS
Library Technician/399312/STSOL/VETASSESS
Life Science Technician/311413/STSOL/VETASSESS
Life Scientist (General)/234511/MLTSSL/VETASSESS
Life Scientists nec/234599/MLTSSL/VETASSESS
Lift Mechanic/341113/MLTSSL/TRA
Livestock Farmers nec/121399/STSOL/VETASSESS
Locksmith/323313/MLTSSL/TRA
Maintenance Planner/312911/Regional/VETASSESS
Make Up Artist/399514/STSOL/TRA
Management Accountant/221112/MLTSSL/CAANZ/CPAA/IPA
Management Consultant/224711/MLTSSL/VETASSESS
Manufacturer/133411/STSOL/VETASSESS
Marine Biologist/234516/MLTSSL/VETASSESS
Market Research Analyst/225112/Regional/VETASSESS
Marketing Specialist/225113/STSOL/VETASSESS
Massage Therapist/411611/STSOL/VETASSESS
Materials Engineer/233112/MLTSSL/Engineers Australia
Mathematician/224112/STSOL/VETASSESS
Meat Inspector/311312/STSOL/VETASSESS
Mechanical Engineer/233512/MLTSSL/Engineers Australia
Mechanical Engineering Draftsperson/312511/Regional/Engineers Australia
Mechanical Engineering Technician/312512/STSOL/TRA
Medical Administrator/134211/Regional/VETASSESS

Medical Diagnostic Radiographer/251211/MLTSSL/ASMIRT
Medical Laboratory Scientist/234611/MLTSSL/AIMS
Medical Laboratory Technician/311213/STSOL/AIMS
Medical Oncologist/253314/MLTSSL/MedBA
Medical Practitioners nec/253999/MLTSSL/MedBA
Medical Radiation Therapist/251212/MLTSSL/ASMIRT
Medical Technicians nec/311299/STSOL/VETASSESS
Metal Fabricator/322311/MLTSSL/TRA
Metal Fitters and Machinists nec/323299/STSOL/TRA
Metal Machinist (First Class)/323214/MLTSSL/TRA
Metallurgical or Materials Technician/312912/STSOL/VETASSESS
Metallurgist/234912/MLTSSL/VETASSESS
Meteorologist/234913/MLTSSL/VETASSESS
Microbiologist/234517/MLTSSL/VETASSESS
Middle School Teacher/241311/STSOL/AITSL
Midwife/254111/MLTSSL/ANMAC
Mine Deputy/312913/STSOL/VETASSESS
Mining Engineer (excluding Petroleum)/233611/MLTSSL/Engineers Australia
Minister of Religion/272211/STSOL/VETASSESS
Mixed Crop and Livestock Farmer/121411/STSOL/VETASSESS
Mixed Crop Farmer/121216/STSOL/VETASSESS
Mixed Livestock Farmer/121317/STSOL/VETASSESS
Motor Mechanic (General)/321211/MLTSSL/TRA
Motorcycle Mechanic/321213/MLTSSL/TRA
Multimedia Designer/232413/Regional/VETASSESS
Multimedia Specialist/261211/MLTSSL/ACS
Music Director/211212/STSOL/VETASSESS
Music Professionals nec/211299/STSOL/VETASSESS
Music Teacher (Private Tuition)/249214/STSOL/VETASSESS
Musician (Instrumental)/211213/MLTSSL/VETASSESS
Natural and Physical Science Professionals nec/234999/MLTSSL/VETASSESS
Naturopath/252213/STSOL/VETASSESS
Naval Architect/233916/MLTSSL/Engineers Australia
Network Administrator/263112/STSOL/ACS
Network Analyst/263113/STSOL/ACS
Neurologist/253318/MLTSSL/MedBA
Neurosurgeon/253513/MLTSSL/MedBA
Newspaper or Periodical Editor/212412/STSOL/VETASSESS
Nuclear Medicine Technologist/251213/MLTSSL/ANZSNM
Nurse Educator/254211/STSOL/ANMAC
Nurse Manager/254311/STSOL/ANMAC

Nurse Practitioner/254411/MLTSSL/ANMAC
Nurse Researcher/254212/STSOL/ANMAC
Nurseryperson/362411/Regional/TRA
Nursing Clinical Director/134212/MLTSSL/ANMAC
Nutritionist/251112/STSOL/VETASSESS
Obstetrician and Gynaecologist/253913/MLTSSL/MedBA
Occupational Health and Safety Adviser/251312/STSOL/VETASSESS
Occupational Therapist/252411/MLTSSL/OTC
Operating Theatre Technician/311214/Regional/VETASSESS
Ophthalmologist/253914/MLTSSL/MedBA
Optometrist/251411/MLTSSL/OCANZ
Organisation and Methods Analyst/224712/STSOL/VETASSESS
Organisational Psychologist/272313/MLTSSL/APS
Orthopaedic Surgeon/253514/MLTSSL/MedBA
Orthoptist/251412/STSOL/VETASSESS
Orthotist or Prosthetist/251912/MLTSSL/AOPA
Osteopath/252112/MLTSSL/AOAC
Other Spatial Scientist/232214/MLTSSL/VETASSESS
Other Sports Coach or Instructor/452317/STSOL/VETASSESS
Otorhinolaryngologist/253515/MLTSSL/MedBA
Paediatric Surgeon/253516/MLTSSL/MedBA
Paediatrician/253321/MLTSSL/MedBA
Painting Trades Worker/332211/MLTSSL/TRA
Panelbeater/324111/MLTSSL/TRA
Pastrycook/351112/STSOL/TRA
Patents Examiner/224914/STSOL/VETASSESS
Pathologist/253915/MLTSSL/MedBA
Pathology Collector/311216/Regional/AIMS
Performing Arts Technicians nec/399599/STSOL/VETASSESS
Petroleum Engineer/233612/MLTSSL/Engineers Australia
Pharmacy Technician/311215/STSOL/VETASSESS
Photographer/211311/STSOL/VETASSESS
Physicist ^/234914/MLTSSL/VETASSESS (non-medical physicist) / ACPSEM (medical physicists)
Physiotherapist/252511/MLTSSL/APC
Pig Farmer/121318/STSOL/VETASSESS
Plastic and Reconstructive Surgeon/253517/MLTSSL/MedBA
Plumber (General)/334111/MLTSSL/TRA
Podiatrist/252611/MLTSSL/APodA/ANZPAC
Policy Analyst/224412/Regional/VETASSESS
Policy and Planning Manager/132411/Regional/VETASSESS
Post Office Manager/142115/Regional/VETASSESS
Poultry Farmer/121321/STSOL/VETASSESS

Power Generation Plant Operator/399213/STSOL/TRA
Precision Instrument Maker and Repairer/323314/STSOL/TRA
Pressure Welder/322312/MLTSSL/TRA
Primary Health Organisation Manager/134213/MLTSSL/VETASSESS
Primary Products Inspectors nec/311399/STSOL/VETASSESS
Primary School Teacher/241213/STSOL/AITSL
Print Finisher/392111/STSOL/TRA
Print Journalist/212413/STSOL/VETASSESS
Printing Machinist/392311/STSOL/TRA
Private Tutors and Teachers nec/249299/STSOL/VETASSESS
Procurement Manager/133612/Regional/AIM
Production Manager (Forestry)/133511/STSOL/VETASSESS
Production Manager (Manufacturing)/133512/STSOL/VETASSESS
Production Manager (Mining)/133513/STSOL/VETASSESS
Production or Plant Engineer/233513/MLTSSL/Engineers Australia
Program Director (Television or Radio)/212315/STSOL/VETASSESS
Program or Project Administrator/511112/STSOL/VETASSESS
Project Builder/133112/Regional/VETASSESS
Property Manager/612112/Regional/VETASSESS
Psychiatrist/253411/MLTSSL/MedBA
Psychologists nec/272399/MLTSSL/APS
Psychotherapist/272314/STSOL/VETASSESS
Public Relations Manager/131114/Regional/AIM
Public Relations Professional/225311/STSOL/VETASSESS
Quality Assurance Manager/139914/STSOL/VETASSESS
Quantity Surveyor/233213/MLTSSL/AIQS
Radiation Oncologist/253918/MLTSSL/MedBA
Radiocommunications Technician/313211/MLTSSL/TRA
Real Estate Representative/612115/Regional/VETASSESS
Records Manager/224214/STSOL/VETASSESS
Recreation Officer/272612/STSOL/VETASSESS
Recruitment Consultant/223112/STSOL/VETASSESS
Regional Education Manager/134412/Regional/VETASSESS
Registered Nurse (Aged Care)/254412/MLTSSL/ANMAC
Registered Nurse (Child and Family Health)/254413/MLTSSL/ANMAC
Registered Nurse (Community Health)/254414/MLTSSL/ANMAC
Registered Nurse (Critical Care and Emergency)/254415/MLTSSL/ANMAC
Registered Nurse (Developmental Disability)/254416/MLTSSL/ANMAC
Registered Nurse (Disability and Rehabilitation)/254417/MLTSSL/ANMAC
Registered Nurse (Medical Practice)/254421/MLTSSL/ANMAC

Registered Nurse (Medical)/254418/MLTSSL/ANMAC
Registered Nurse (Mental Health)/254422/MLTSSL/ANMAC
Registered Nurse (Paediatrics)/254425/MLTSSL/ANMAC
Registered Nurse (Perioperative)/254423/MLTSSL/ANMAC
Registered Nurse (Surgical)/254424/MLTSSL/ANMAC
Registered Nurses nec/254499/MLTSSL/ANMAC
Rehabilitation Counsellor/272114/STSOL/VETASSESS
Renal Medicine Specialist/253322/MLTSSL/MedBA
Research and Development Manager/132511/STSOL/VETASSESS
Resident Medical Officer/253112/STSOL/MedBA
Residential Care Officer/411715/STSOL/VETASSESS
Retail Buyer/639211/STSOL/VETASSESS
Retail Pharmacist/251513/STSOL/APharmC
Rheumatologist/253323/MLTSSL/MedBA
Roof Plumber/334115/MLTSSL/TRA
Roof Tiler/333311/STSOL/TRA
Safety Inspector/312611/Regional/VETASSESS
Sales and Marketing Manager/131112/STSOL/AIM
School Principal/134311/STSOL/VETASSESS
Science Technicians nec/311499/STSOL/VETASSESS
Secondary School Teacher/241411/MLTSSL/AITSL
Sheep Farmer/121322/STSOL/VETASSESS
Sheetmetal Trades Worker/322211/MLTSSL/TRA
Ship's Master/231213/Regional/AMSA
Shipwright/399112/MLTSSL/TRA
Signwriter/399611/STSOL/TRA
Small Engine Mechanic/321214/MLTSSL/TRA
Snowsport Instructor/452314/STSOL/VETASSESS
Social Professionals nec/272499/STSOL/VETASSESS
Social Worker/272511/MLTSSL/AASW
Software and Applications Programmers nec/261399/MLTSSL/ACS
Software Engineer/261313/MLTSSL/ACS
Software Tester/261314/STSOL/ACS
Solicitor/271311/MLTSSL/A legal admissions authority of a State or Territory
Solid Plasterer/333212/MLTSSL/TRA
Sonographer/251214/MLTSSL/ASMIRT
Sound Technician/399516/STSOL/TRA
Special Education Teachers nec/241599/MLTSSL/AITSL
Special Needs Teacher/241511/MLTSSL/AITSL
Specialist Managers nec/139999/STSOL/VETASSESS
Specialist Physician (General Medicine)/253311/MLTSSL/MedBA
Specialist Physicians nec/253399/MLTSSL/MedBA

Speech Pathologist/252712/MLTSSL/SPA
Sports Administrator/139915/Regional/VETASSESS
Sports Centre Manager/149113/Regional/VETASSESS
Sports Development Officer/452321/STSOL/VETASSESS
Sportspersons nec/452499/STSOL/VETASSESS
Stage Manager/212316/STSOL/VETASSESS
Statistician/224113/MLTSSL/VETASSESS
Stockbroking Dealer/222213/STSOL/VETASSESS
Stonemason/331112/MLTSSL/TRA
Structural Engineer/233214/MLTSSL/Engineers Australia
Student Counsellor/272115/STSOL/VETASSESS
Sugar Cane Grower/121217/STSOL/VETASSESS
Supply and Distribution Manager/133611/STSOL/AIM
Surgeon (General)/253511/MLTSSL/MedBA
Surveying or Spatial Science Technician/312116/Regional/VETASSESS
Surveyor/232212/MLTSSL/SSSI
Swimming Coach or Instructor/452315/STSOL/VETASSESS
Systems Administrator/262113/STSOL/ACS
Systems Analyst/261112/MLTSSL/ACS
Taxation Accountant/221113/MLTSSL/CAANZ/CPAA/IPA
Teacher of English to Speakers of Other Languages/249311/STSOL/ VETASSESS
Teacher of the Hearing Impaired/241512/MLTSSL/AITSL
Teacher of the Sight Impaired/241513/MLTSSL/AITSL
Technical Cable Jointer/342212/MLTSSL/TRA
Technical Director/212317/STSOL/VETASSESS
Technical Sales Representatives nec/225499/STSOL/VETASSESS
Technical Writer/212415/STSOL/VETASSESS
Telecommunications Engineer/263311/MLTSSL/Engineers Australia
Telecommunications Field Engineer/313212/MLTSSL/Engineers Australia
Telecommunications Linesworker/342413/STSOL/TRA
Telecommunications Network Engineer/263312/MLTSSL/ Engineers Australia
Telecommunications Network Planner/313213/MLTSSL/ Engineers Australia
Telecommunications Technical Officer or Technologist/313214/MLTSSL/ Engineers Australia
Television Journalist/212416/STSOL/VETASSESS
Tennis Coach/452316/STSOL/VETASSESS
Textile, Clothing and Footwear Mechanic/323215/STSOL/TRA
Thoracic Medicine Specialist/253324/MLTSSL/MedBA

Toolmaker/323412/STSOL/TRA
Traditional Chinese Medicine Practitioner/252214/STSOL/Chinese Medicine Board of Australia
Translator/272413/Regional/NAATI
Transport Company Manager/149413/STSOL/VETASSESS
Transport Engineer/233215/MLTSSL/Engineers Australia
University Lecturer/242111/MLTSSL/VETASSESS
Upholsterer/393311/STSOL/TRA
Urban and Regional Planner/232611/STSOL/VETASSESS
Urologist/253518/MLTSSL/MedBA
Valuer/224512/MLTSSL/VETASSESS
Vascular Surgeon/253521/MLTSSL/MedBA
Vegetable Grower/121221/STSOL/VETASSESS
Vehicle Body Builder/324211/STSOL/TRA
Vehicle Painter/324311/Regional/TRA
Vehicle Trimmer/324212/STSOL/TRA
Veterinarian/234711/MLTSSL/AVBC
Veterinary Nurse/361311/STSOL/VETASSESS
Video Producer/212318/STSOL/VETASSESS
Visual Arts and Crafts Professionals nec/211499/STSOL/VETASSESS
Vocational Education Teacher/242211/Regional/VETASSESS
Wall and Floor Tiler/333411/MLTSSL/TRA
Watch and Clock Maker and Repairer/323316/STSOL/TRA
Web Administrator/313113/STSOL/ACS
Web Designer/232414/STSOL/VETASSESS
Web Developer/261212/STSOL/ACS
Welder (First Class)/322313/MLTSSL/TRA
Welfare Centre Manager/134214/MLTSSL/ACWA
Welfare Worker/272613/STSOL/ACWA
Wine Maker/234213/Regional/VETASSESS
Wood Machinist/394213/STSOL/TRA
Wood Machinists and Other Wood Trades Workers nec/394299/STSOL/TRA
Workplace Relations Adviser/223113/Regional/VETASSESS
Youth Worker/411716/STSOL/ACWA
Zookeeper/361114/Regional/VETASSESS

Factsheet 2.2 Points Test Table

Age	18-24		25
	25-32		30
	33-39		25
	40-44		15
	45-49		0
Qualification	Doctorate		20
	At least an undergraduate degree		15
	Diploma/ trade qualification		10
Experience (maximum. 20 points)	Australian Work Experience	<1 year	0
		≥1 but < 3 years	5
		≥3 but < 5 years	10
		≥5 but ≤ 8 years	15
		≥8 and up to 10 years	20
	Overseas Work Experience	< 3 years	0
		≥ 3 but < 5 years	5
		≥ 5 but < 8 year	10
		≥8 and up to 10 years	15
English language	Competent		0
	Proficient		10
	Superior		20
Nomination/ sponsorship	Nominated by state or territory government or sponsored by an eligible family member, to reside and work in a specified /designated area (for visa subclass 489 only)		10
	Nominated by state or territory government (visa subclass 190 only)		5
Others	Credential community language qualifications		5
	Study in regional Australia or a low population growth metropolitan area (distance education excluded)		5
	Partner skill qualifications		5
	Professional Year[3] in Australia for at least 1 year in the previous 4 years		5
	Australia educational qualification		5
	Specialist education qualification		5
	Accredited Para-professional interpreter or translator		5
Partner's skill and qualification	Age < 50, competent English, positive skill assessment		5

Factsheet 2.3 Australian Values Statement

The Australian values statement for permanent or provisional visa applications is as follow:

I confirm that I have read, or had explained to me, information provided by the Australian Government on Australian society and values.

I understand:

- Australian society values respect for the freedom and dignity of the individual, freedom of religion, commitment to the rule of law, Parliamentary democracy, equality of men and women and a spirit of egalitarianism that embraces mutual respect, tolerance, fair play and compassion for those in need and pursuit of the public good
- Australian society values equality of opportunity for individuals, regardless of their race, religion or ethnic background
- The English language, as the national language, is an important unifying element of Australian society.

I undertake to respect these values of Australian society during my stay in Australia and to obey the laws of Australia.

I understand that, if I should seek to become an Australian citizen:

- Australian citizenship is a shared identity, a common bond which unites all Australians while respecting their diversity
- Australian citizenship involves reciprocal rights and responsibilities. The responsibilities of Australian Citizenship include obeying Australian laws, including those relating to voting at elections and serving on a jury.

If I meet the legal qualifications for becoming an Australian citizen and my application is approved I understand that I would have to pledge my loyalty to Australia and its people.

Source: Department of Home Affairs, Australia

Factsheet 3.1 Skills Assessing Authorities

AACAA - Architects Accreditation Council of Australia
AASW - Australian Society of Social Workers
ACPSEM - Australasian College of Physical Scientists And Engineers in Medicine
ACS - Australian Computer Society
AIM - Australian Institute of Management
AIMS - Australian Institute of Medical Scientists
AIQS - Australian Institute of Quantity Surveyors
AIR - Australian Institute of Radiography
AITSL - Australia Institute for Teaching and School Leadership
AMSA - Australian Maritime Safety Authority
ANMAC - Australian Nursing & Midwifery Accreditation Council
ANZOC - Australasian Osteopathic Accreditation Council (AOAC)
ANZSNM - Australian and New Zealand Society of Nuclear Medicine
ANZPAC - The Australian and New Zealand Podiatry Accreditation Council
APC - Australian Physiotherapy Council
APharmC - Australian Pharmacy Council
APS - Australian Psychological Society
AVBC - Australasian Veterinary Boards Council
CASA - Civil Aviation Safety Authority
CCEA - The Council on Chiropractic Education Australasia
Chinese Medicine Board of Australia - Chinese Medicine Board of Australia
CPA - CPA Australia
Engineers Australia - Engineers Australia
ICAA - Chartered Accountants Australia and New Zealand
IPA - Institute of Public Accountants
Medical Board of Australia - Medical Board of Australia
NAATI - National Accreditation Authority for Translators and Interpreters
OCANZ - The Optometry Council of Australia and New Zealand
OTC - Occupational Therapist Council
SLAA - State Legal Admission Authority (SLAA)
SPA - Speech Pathology Australia
SSSI - Surveying & Spatial Sciences Institute
VETASSESS – VETASSESS

Factsheet 4.1 Occupation Ceilings 2018-19

Example:
Accountants 2211-3753

Occupation - Accountants

ANSCO Occupation Group Code - 2211

Occupation Ceiling - 3753 places

Accountants*/2211-3753

Actuaries, Mathematicians and Statisticians/2241-1000

Agricultural and Forestry Scientists/2341-1000

Airconditioning and Refrigeration Mechanics/3421-1836

Architects and Landscape Architects/2321-1251

Auditors, Company Secretaries and Corporate Treasurers*/2212-1342

Automotive Electricians/3211-1000

Barristers/2711-1000

Boat Builders and Shipwrights/3991-1000

Bricklayers and Stonemasons/3311-1594

Cabinetmakers/3941-1421

Carpenters and Joiners/3312-8372

Cartographers and Surveyors/2322-1000

Chefs/3513-2821

Chemical and Materials Engineers/2331-1000

Child Care Centre Managers/1341-1000

Chiropractors and Osteopaths/2521-1000

Civil Engineering Draftspersons and Technicians/3122-1000

Civil Engineering Professionals/2332-3510

Computer Network Professionals*/2631-2167

Construction Managers/1331-5982

Database and Systems Administrators and ICT Security Specialists/2621-2660

Early Childhood (Pre-primary School) Teachers/2411-2488

Electrical Distribution Trades Workers/3422-1019

Electrical Engineering Draftspersons and Technicians/3123-1000

Electrical Engineers/2333-1000

Electricians/3411-9303

Electronics Engineers*/2334-300

Electronics Trades Workers/3423-1769

Engineering Managers/1332-1131

General Practitioners and Resident Medical officers/2531-3348

Glaziers/3331-1000

Health and Welfare Services Managers/1342-1302

ICT Business and Systems Analysts*/2611-1466

Industrial, Mechanical and Production Engineers*/2335-1780

Internal Medicine Specialists/2533-1000

Land Economists and Valuers/2245-1000

Livestock Farmers/1213-4841

Management consultant/2247-3894

Medical Imaging Professionals/2512-1224

Medical Laboratory Scientists/2346-1600

Metal Fitters and Machinists/3232-6989

Midwives/2541-1000

Motor Mechanics/3212-6099

Occupational Therapists/2524-1227

Optometrists and Orthoptists/2514-1000

Other Engineering Professionals*/2339-700

Other Health Diagnostic and Promotion Professionals/2519-1000

Other Medical Practitioners/2539-1145

Other Natural and Physical Science Professionals/2349-1000

Painting Trades Workers/3322-3277

Panelbeaters/3241-1000

Physiotherapists/2525-1613

Plasterers/3332-2081

Plumbers/3341-5766

Podiatrists/2526-1000

Precision Metal Trades Workers/3233-1000

Psychiatrists/2534-1000

Psychologists/2723-2228

Registered Nurses/2544-17322

Secondary School Teachers/2414-8480

Sheetmetal Trades Workers/3222-1000

Social Workers/2725-2125

Software and Applications Programmers*/2613-7271

Solicitors/2713-3770

Special Education Teachers/2415-1000

Speech Professionals and Audiologists/2527-1000

Factsheet 5.1 Personal, Relationship Information & Documents

Visa applicant's personal information	- Identification page of passport (photo, name and date of birth) or birth certificate - A national identity card, if available - Proof of change of name if applicable - A marriage or divorce certificate - Change of name documents from an Australian registry of births, deaths and marriages, or the relevant overseas authority - Documents that show other names applicant has been known by
Relationship with other family members	Personal information Birth Certificate (requirements for both applicant and family member); Marriage Certificate; Proof of Name Change; Official Relationship Certificate if applicable
	Relationship documents Persons who have been married, widowed, divorced or permanently separated, provide proof such as divorce documents, death certificates, separation documents or statutory declarations.

Factsheet 5.2 Skills, Qualification, Experience, English Proficiency & Skills Assessments

Nominated occupation	ANSCO code
Work experience	Letter(s) from current and previous employer(s), confirming commencement date, job title, duties and tasks, salary and number of hours worked per week, for all skilled work experience in Australia. Employment references on company letterhead and signed by the author detailing: • Start & finish dates of employment • Description of duties performed required to determine the relevance to the nominated occupation • Hours worked • Full time or part time • Country where employment was completed

Education and training	• Academic transcript and graduation certificate and/or letter of completion from an overseas institution* or
	• Australian institution with the following information detailed in the qualification documents:
	   - title of degree or award
	   - name of university or awarding institution
	   - date the degree or award was completed
	   - unit or subject names and grades or marks achieved
	   - abstract of research if the qualification has been completed through research
	
	* The qualification must be recognised as being equivalent to an Australian Bachelor degree or higher.

English language proficiency	English Test certificate English Language Tests must be less than three years old. For Cambridge English, advanced tests must have been taken on or after 01/01/2015.
Skills assessment	Positive skills assessment assessed by the relevant skills assessing authority for the main applicant's nominated occupation. Qualification assessment if applicable.

Factsheet 5.3 Health & Character Requirements

Health requirements

- Person aged <2 years

  Medical examination

- Person aged ≥2 but <11 years

  Medical examination and TB Screening test (TST or IGRA) if coming from a higher risk country for TB

- Person aged ≥11 but <15 years

  Medical examination and chest x-ray

- Person aged ≥15

  Medical examination, chest x-ray and HIV test

Character requirements

- National Police Certificate issued by the Australian police certificate for persons who have spent a total of 12 months or more in Australia in the last 10 years since turning 16. **Australian police certificates are valid for 12 months from the date of issue for this purpose.**
- Overseas police certificate from every country, including applicant's home country, where applicant has spent a total of 12 months or more in the last 10 years since turning 16
- **Military service records or discharge papers if applicant has served in the armed forces of any country**

Factsheet 5.4 Partner's Documents

Partner

- Identity documents
- Character documents
- Marriage certificate, if applicable
- Documents about other relationships, if applicable

For de facto relationships

Provide either:

- Evidence that the relationship is registered by an Australian State or
- Enough documents to prove the de facto relationship has been for at least 12 months prior to visa application

Evidence of genuine and continuing relationship

For both married and de facto applicants evidence that the applicant is in a genuine and continuing relationship. Evidence can include but is not limited to:

- Joint bank account statements
- Billing accounts in joint names
- Joint leases or mortgages
- Documents that showing the couple has lived at the same address

Proof of applicant's partner has functional English

No documentary proof of partner's functional English required if applicant's partner is a citizen of and holds a valid passport from United Kingdom, Republic of Ireland, United States, Canada and New Zealand.

If applicant can't show the partner has functional English, applicant will need to pay the second instalment of the visa application charge when asked to do.

Factsheet 5.5 Dependents Under 18 - Documentary Proof

Each dependent included in application	• Identity documents • Character documents, if applicable

Parental responsibility documents	Applicant must get consent for a dependent child to migrate to Australia from anyone who:
	• Has a legal right to decide where the dependent lives and
	• Is not coming to australia with the dependent
	• They must complete either:
	  - Form 1229 Consent form to grant an Australian visa to a child under the age of 18 years
	  - statutory declaration giving their consent for the child to migrate to Australia on this visa

Person completing the form or making the statutory declaration	A document with the contact details, signature and photo passport and driver's licence, or Provide evidence that the applicant has the legal right to determine where the dependent child lives, e.g. a court order.

Factsheet 5.6 Dependents Over 18 – Documentary Proof

Each dependent included in application	• Identity documents • Character documents, if applicable
Proof od dependency	• A completed form 47a details of a child or other dependent family member aged 18 years or over • Proof of applicant's relationship with the dependent such as a birth certificate or adoption papers
Proof of financial dependency (for at least 12 months before the application)	• Proof they live with the applicant • Their tax records • Proof they are currently studying If the dependent has turned 23 on the date DHA makes a decision on their application applicant must also provide evidence that they are wholly or substantially reliant on the applicant or applicant's partner for financial support because they are incapacitated for work due to the total or partial loss of their bodily or mental functions.
Proof of functional English by applicant's dependents	• No documentary proof of dependent has functional English required if applicant's dependent is a citizen of and holds a valid passport from the United Kingdom, the Republic of Ireland, the United States, Canada or New Zealand. • If applicant can't show the dependent has functional English, applicant will need to pay the second instalment of the visa application charge when asked to do.

Factsheet 5.7 Skills Assessment Documentary Proof

Medical practitioners	One of these certificates issued by the Australian Health Practitioner Regulation Agency: • Unconditional or general medical registration • Conditional specialist registration – which allows applicant to practice only in applicant's specialty with no further training or supervision requirements Applicant must be registered at the time of invitation to apply.
Barristers and solicitors	Proof of admission to practice as a lawyer in the relevant Australian state or territory. Applicant must be registered at the time of invitation to apply.
Others	A copy of applicant's skills assessment documents.

Factsheet 5.8 Expression of Interest Documentary Proof

Documents proof all of the claims (if applicable) applicant made in the EOI:

- Skills assessment
- English language skills
- Skilled employment
- Qualifications
- Australian study requirement
- State or territory government agency nomination
- Specialist education requirement
- Accredited community language
- Study in regional Australia
- Partner skills
- Professional year in Australia

Factsheet 5.9 Non-English Documents & Document Scanning

Translation of Non-English documents	All non-English documents have to be translated into English by translator accredited by the National Accreditation Authority for Translators and Interpreters. For translation by translators (accreditation not required) outside Australia, each translation must include the following details of the translator: • Full name • Address and telephone number • Qualifications and experience in the language they are translating
Scan or photograph	Scan or photograph all documents (English and non-English) must be in colour. For document exceeding one page, save all as one file.

Factsheet 5.10 If Applicant is getting Help

Applicant needs to inform DHA if applicant is getting help:

- ❖ Form 956a re appointment or withdrawal of an authorised recipient of applicant's correspondence
- ❖ Form 956 re advice by a migration agent/exempt person of providing immigration assistance
- ❖ Inform DHA in writing (upload in ImmiAccount) re persons acting for the applicant but not providing immigration assistance and detail what they can do on applicant's behalf (e.g. submit or withdraw an application for applicant).

About the Author

Ng Chee Min has lived in Australia for over 32 years.

He has an economics degree and a Masters degree in Business. He is also a professional accountant, having qualified as a member of two professional accounting bodies in the United Kingdom and two more in Australia.

His professional career in Malaysia and Australia over four decades includes CFO and CEO roles in the private sector and advisory roles in the public sector. He has taught at university and presented at numerous seminars and conferences both in Australia and overseas.

His first book on Australian migration program was published in late 2013. He has since written several more books on the subject.

www.ingramcontent.com/pod-product-compliance
Lightning Source LLC
Chambersburg PA
CBHW071126030426
42336CB00013BA/2223